INVITING SCHOOL SUCCESS
A Self-Concept Approach
to Teaching and Learning

William Watson Purkey
University of North Carolina at Greensboro

Wadsworth Publishing Company, Inc.
Belmont, California

Printed in the United States of America

3 4 5 6 7 8 9 10—82 81 80 79

Library of Congress Cataloging in Publication Data

Purkey, William Watson.
  Inviting school success.

  Bibliography: p.
  Includes index.
  1. Teaching. 2. Teacher-student relationships.
I. Title.
LB1025.2.P89 371.1′02 77-13601
ISBN 0-534-00566-7

Education Editor: Roger Peterson

Production Editor: Anne Kelly

Designer: Ann Wilkinson

Cover Photographer: Elizabeth Crews

Acknowledgments

The excerpt on page 67 is reprinted with permission of Macmillan Publishing Co., Inc. and Jonathan Cape Ltd. from *Manchild in the Promised Land* by Claude Brown. Copyright © 1965 by Claude Brown.

The excerpt on pages 68—69 is reprinted with permission of Allyn & Bacon, Inc. from *Helping Relationships: Basic Concepts for the Helping Professions* by A. Combs, D. Avila, and W. Purkey, Allyn & Bacon, Inc., 1971.

The excerpt on page 14 is reprinted with permission of E. P. Dutton & Co., Inc. and Curtis Brown Limited from *Nigger: An Autobiography* by Dick Gregory, with Robert Lipsyte. Copyright © 1964 by Dick Gregory Enterprises, Inc.

Though her mien carries much more invitation than command,
To behold her is an immediate check to loose behavior;
To love her is a liberal education.

Tatler No. 49
1709—1711

CONTENTS

Several years ago I wrote a book that explored the positive, persistent relationship between various dimensions of self-concept and school achievement (*Self-Concept and School Achievement,* Englewood-Cliffs, N.J.: Prentice-Hall, 1970). That earlier book presented research-based evidence to support the thesis that each student's subjective, personal evaluation of his or her unique existence significantly relates to the student's success or failure in school. While conclusions remain tentative (it is risky to assume simple causal relationships in an interrelated, open system), the research emerging since 1970 continues to support my original thesis.

Following the appearance of the earlier book, many people contacted me to ask such questions as: "Assuming that self-concept does play an important role in school achievement, how can we build a student's self-concept?" "What can our school do to enhance students' self-esteem?" "What can we do to make self-concept an important part of our school curriculum?" In response to these questions, I have written this book, **INVITING SCHOOL SUCCESS.**

INVITING SCHOOL SUCCESS approaches its subject from a humanistic viewpoint. Compared with other approaches to teaching that view teachers as "managers," "motivators," "shapers," "researchers," "consultants," "counselors," or "guides," this approach defines the teacher as *inviter.* This book describes good teaching as the process of inviting students to see themselves as able, valuable, and self-directing and of encouraging them to act in accordance with these self-perceptions.

Rather than viewing students as physical objects to be moved about like puppets on strings, the teacher's primary role is to see students in essentially positive ways and to invite them to behave accordingly. Students, like all of us, greatly benefit from others who see and communicate to them the positive traits and potentials that they may not see in themselves. "In my junior year of high school," a student wrote, "my favorite teacher and I engaged in a discussion about the girls and boys most likely to be nominated for student council president. My choices were two of my very good friends. The teacher and I agreed that my two friends were highly qualified, but then she asked 'And what about you?' I remember thinking this was hilarious; I couldn't picture me in that role. Still, she insisted that I had the same qualities as my friends. Much later, she told me she was not a bit surprised when

I was elected student council president." Invitations, as we will see, bid us to grow and to realize our human potential.

At this point, we cannot guarantee that students will learn more or be happier in an inviting school environment. However, research on *invitational teaching* (teaching that corresponds with the model presented in this book) has begun (Inglis, 1976; Purkey, 1975, 1976a, 1976b). This research, plus the anecdotal reports of over two thousand students at various grade levels, reveal that what students remember about "good teachers" are the invitations to learning sent by these teachers. What they remember about "bad teachers" are the ways these teachers disinvited students. "It's terrible," wrote one fourth-grader, "when Mrs. Reed is picking on me, and everything is missing, and tears are rolling down my eyes." Judging by what we now know about school life, an invitational approach to education very likely increases the probability of student success and happiness in the classroom.

Because this book stresses the importance of school success, it may be viewed as advocating a "basics approach" to education. Such a view is correct insofar as it emphasizes the importance of academic achievement. At the same time, the invitational approach is anchored in an unconditional commitment to the value, ability, and self-directing powers of the individual student. In light of a growing emphasis on the *factory model* of education characterized by a mechanistic orientation—the view of students and teachers as functionaries, with a primary emphasis on product—the need for an invitational approach to education has never been greater.

INVITING SCHOOL SUCCESS begins with a definition of *invitations,* an explanation of the nature of invitations found in schools, and a description of the teacher's power to send invitations. The opening chapters describe the formal and informal, verbal and nonverbal, witting and unwitting ways in which students are powerfully "invited" or "disinvited" in their school careers. Using recent research findings regarding the importance of self-concept, these chapters present arguments that favor an invitational approach to teaching and learning.

The middle chapters describe the importance of the teacher's positive view of students and offer ways to put these views into classroom practice. While almost everyone extends invitations from time to time, those sent by invitational teachers reflect particular beliefs about themselves, others, and the world. Their invitations are intentional, developed to high proficiency by practice and experience, and delivered with special skill. These teachers maintain respect for students and responsibility for the invitations they extend. As one student wrote, "Miss Penn invited us to like ourselves and to take pride in our work. She expected a great deal of us, and we did not let her down."

The concluding chapters focus on specific ways to invite learning. The Florida Key (Purkey, Cage, and Graves, 1973) provides a basis to explore four ingredients of a positive self-concept as learner. The final chapter presents the concept of the invitational school. This school is based on a *family model,* characterized by warmth, cooperative spirit, and positive expectations.

I have written **INVITING SCHOOL SUCCESS** so it can be useful in various courses, such as methods, curriculum, educational psychology, foundations of education, and introduction to education. Its small size and compact nature will appeal to teachers in training at both graduate and undergraduate levels, also to professionals in schools of teacher education as well as those in actual daily contact with students. These include principals, supervisors, counselors, school psychologists—and all helpers who wish to improve the quality of education for all students.

These are some of the people who contributed the most to my understanding of invitations: my wife, Imogene Hedrick Purkey, who twenty-six years ago accepted my invitation to spend our lives together; my high-school teachers, Mrs. Field, Miss Penn, and Mr. Johnson, who saw things that others missed; my University of Virginia professors, Richard Beard and Virgil Ward, who invited me to grow intellectually; my friends Hal Altmann, Richard Aubry, Don Avila, Lee Bard, Charles Branch, Walter Busby, Art Combs, Sandi Damico, Mike Fagan, Cheryl Gowie, Sandi Inglis, Alan Kirby, Pam Leary, Hal Lewis, Don McFayden, John Novak, Frank Pajaras, Betty and Joel Siegel, Earl and Lynda Varnes, Mark Wasicsko, Hannelore Wass, and Harry Wong—among others who were and are the source of countless invitations . . . many thanks.

I am grateful also to Richard Coop, University of North Carolina at Chapel Hill; Frank R. Cross, Oregon State University; Jack Schmidt, University of North Carolina at Greensboro; Todd Shirley, Iowa State University;

and Thomas Ringness, University of Wisconsin. Their reviews enabled me to penetrate deeply into the world of invitations.

On a personal note, my excitement and enthusiasm as I wrote this book would be difficult to overestimate. I wholeheartedly invite you to share these ideas and validate them against your own relationships with students of all ages. I hope you will find yourself agreeing with the third-grader who wrote, "I like *enventasions!*"

William Watson Purkey

1　　TEACHING IS
INVITING

*I now believe there is no biological, geographical,
social, economic, or psychological determiner of
man's condition that he cannot transcend if he is
suitably invited or challenged to do so.*

Sidney Jourard *Disclosing Man to Himself*
(1968, p. 59)

After generations of study, researchers still lack a systematic way of describing the events of communication between teachers and students that result in learning. Despite literally thousands of research studies, articles, books, and reports about the nature of "good teaching," there is still very little agreement (Brophy and Evertson, 1976; Ellena, Stevenson, and Webb, 1961; Stevenson, 1972; and others).

What actually happens when teaching occurs? Although no one knows the answer to this question, a growing body of research data points to the teacher—his or her attentiveness, expectancies, encouragements, attitudes, and evaluations—as the primary force in influencing students' perceptions of themselves as learners. These teacher characteristics, reflected in their behavior, increase or decrease the probability of student learning (Braun, 1976; Brophy and Good, 1970; Doyle, Hancock, and Kifer, 1972; Lanzetta and Hannah, 1969; Mendels and Flanders, 1973; Palardy, 1969; Purkey, 1970; Rist, 1970; and others). Beyond the "hard" data, countless anecdotal self-reports describe the impact of teacher behavior on student self-concept and success in school. "After completing high school and working on the railroad for a year," a student wrote, "I decided to apply for admission to college. I went to the head of my high-school English Department for a recommendation. I was afraid he would look at me with skepticism, for I was a graduate of the general program. But instead, he looked at me, smiled, and said: 'I was hoping that you would decide to do this.' What an invitation!"

Similar reports and findings on the impact of the behavior of significant others on student self-concept and achievement have also been reported in professions other than teaching. The field of medicine recognizes that certain sicknesses (iatrogenic diseases) can result from the physician's witting or unwitting signals to patients to consider themselves less than healthy (*Dorland's,* 1974). (Can you imagine the impact of a medical doctor's statement to you that "your heart is not as strong as we would like it to be"?) In clinical psychology, it is believed that improved behavior as a result of therapy is primarily due to the attitudinal qualities of the relationship, which encourage a more positive, realistic self-concept in clients (Rogers, 1973; 1974). "It was not what he knew, but who he was, that seemed to help me the most," wrote one client. In mental hospitals, Clark (1974), Farina

(1976), Goffman (1961), Rosenhan (1973), and others have demonstrated that hospital personnel influence patients to conform to contemporary ideas of how mental patients should behave. This phenomenon was dramatized in Ken Kesey's novel *One Flew over the Cuckoo's Nest* (1962). Nurse Ratched kept reminding the other hospital personnel, "This is an institution for the insane. . . . It is important to get patients adjusted to surroundings." Throughout the helping professions, the nature of attitudes reflected in the messages transmitted to others plays a profound role in determining the course of human development.

The basic premise of this book is that teachers and other helpers, for reasons we will explore, perceive students in different ways. These differential perceptions, manifested in the myriad ways that teachers behave toward students, heavily influence students' self-perceptions and their success or failure in school. Recognition of this fact is epitomized by one teacher who commented: "My job is to help children understand how *good* they are and how *much* they can learn."

Although research on the individual effects of attitudes on behavior continues in many professional fields, it is now possible to synthesize the various findings; we can bring into focus the countless, often unrecognized processes whereby students learn to see themselves as responsible, capable, and valuable—or as irresponsible, incapable, and worthless. These self-perceptions, as Felice (1975) Goffman (1959), and others have documented, are basic ingredients in student success or failure.

INVITATIONS IN THE SCHOOL

> *You send strange invitations, Sir!*
>
> **Beauty** Beauty and the Beast

Invitations take countless forms and deal with all areas of human interaction. We are surrounded by invitations, from formal requests to informal urgings, to trust, buy, eat more, eat less, do this, do that, and to develop spiritually, socially, intellectually, and physically. This book is limited to invitations and disinvitations that play a significant role in student success or failure in schools.

As used here, an *invitation* is a summary description of messages—verbal and nonverbal, formal and informal—continuously transmitted to students with the intention of informing them that they are responsible, able, and valuable. Conversely, a *disinvitation* is intended to tell them that they are irresponsible, incapable, and worthless. The word *invitation* has a special value: It indicates both respect for the one invited and responsibility on the part of the inviter. Invitational teaching is a "doing with," rather than a "doing to," process.

For years, educators have been concerned with the apparent lack of communication in schools. Yet the problem is not a failure to communicate, for teachers and students communicate quite well. The problem is *what* is communicated. As we will see, there are different levels of communication, and both teachers and students may be unintentionally disinviting. For example, a teacher's suggestion to play "Simon Says," may be most inviting to a second-grade class, but most disinviting to a high-school class.

An invitation to learning may be as formal as a bronze pin presented at an assembly awards program, an assignment to a "gifted" group, or a note of praise sent to parents. It may also be as informal as a teacher taking special notice of a child's new shoes; as subtle as providing a coughdrop for a nagging cough; or as nonverbal as a smile, a nod, or a wink. Even several seconds of silence ("wait-time") can be most inviting as we will see in Chapter 5.

Invitations and disinvitations in the classroom take many forms. The findings of classroom interaction studies indicate that teachers tend to exhibit more positive nonverbal behavior (smiles, nods, winks) to students considered bright than to those considered "dull" (Chaikin and Sigler, 1973). Teachers also "teach more to," "spend more time with," and "request more from" students they consider to be able (Baker and Crist, 1971). Furthermore, "least efficient" learners are more likely to be ignored (Willis, 1970), to receive less attention (Rothbart, Dalfen and Barrett, 1971), and to be given fewer opportunities to respond (Good, 1970). Based on the image of their ability and potential in the minds of teachers, certain students receive a disproportionate number of invitations to learning, while others are ignored or dissuaded.

The influence of teacher attitudes on student achievement has received considerable attention. Some studies have failed to provide evidence that teacher expectancy influences student performance (Claiborn, 1969; Fielder, Cohen, and Finney, 1971; Fleming and Anttonen, 1971; José and Cody, 1971; Wilkins and Glock, 1973), but most research findings support the view that students are more than likely to perform as their teachers think they will (Clarke, 1960; Cornbleth, David, and Button, 1974; Garner and Bing, 1973; Meichenbaum, Bowers, and Ross, 1969; Mendels and Flanders, 1973; Rist, 1970; Seaver, 1973; Tyo, 1972; and others). As Brophy and Good (1974) concluded from their extensive research: "When teachers had higher expectations for students, they actually produced higher achievement in those students than in students for whom they had lower expectations" (p. 80).

Perhaps the best known study on teacher expectancy is that of Rosenthal and Jacobson (1968a, 1968b), who reported their success in influencing student performance by giving teachers favorable data about selected students. While Rosenthal and Jacobson's research, reported in their book *Pygmalion in the Classroom* (1968b), received criticism for its methodology (Snow, 1969; Taylor, 1970; Thorndike, 1968), critics have not questioned its basic assumption that teacher attitudes influence student performance.

Although conclusions remain tentative, growing evidence indicates that teachers hold different expectations for different students, that these expectations influence teacher behavior, and that this behavior influences student self-perceptions and school achievement (Clark, Corno, Gage, Marx, Peterson, Stayrook, and Winne, 1976; Evans and Rosenthal, 1969; Friedman and Friedman, 1973; Lanzetta, 1969; LaVoie and Adams, 1974; Long and Henderson, 1974; Purkey, 1970; Rosenthal and Rubin, 1971; Woolfolk and Woolfolk, 1974; and others). Brophy and Good (1974) expressed their view of teacher expectations in this statement: "Regardless of where one stands concerning Rosenthal and Jacobson's original data, work by a large number of investigators using a variety of methods over the past several years has established unequivocally that teachers' expectations can and do function as self-fulfilling prophecies, although not always or automatically" (p. 32). The subtle, indirect ways in which a prophecy is fulfilled are reflected in this student's account of a disinvitation: "When I was in the third grade, a choral teacher said I was a good listener. Everyone laughed, except me. I've never uttered a musical note in public from that day to this." Another student might have taken the teacher's remark humorously, but this student took it very seriously.

In addition to the research on teacher expectancy, exploratory studies continue in the areas of teacher belief systems (Combs et al., 1969; Usher and Hanke, 1971; Wasicsko, 1977), teacher attentiveness (Rothbart, Dalfen, and Barrett, 1971); teacher enthusiasm (Rosenshine, 1970), and teacher evaluations (Woolfolk and Woolfolk, 1974). On the basis of this research, it is clear that teachers use both verbal and nonverbal communication systems to signal their attitudes. "My mother and I moved from rural South Carolina to upstate Michigan," a high-school girl wrote. "When I entered the Michigan school, I shyly approached my new teacher. I repeated my name when she failed to understand me the first time. 'Audrey,' the teacher asked, 'where are you from?' 'South Carolina,' I said. 'You see, my father died, and we had to move here.' 'Well, Audrey,' she responded, 'you're in the North now, and you should start speaking like a Northerner.' She didn't care what I had just said about my father." The belief systems of teachers, communicated in their inviting or disinviting behaviors, have a significant impact on student attitudes.

The studies thus far mentioned document the presence of differential teacher expectations and treatment of students; yet they do not explain the factors that prompt these beliefs and behaviors. Although most researchers have focused on teacher attitudes and actions, it is obvious that particular patterns of *student* attitudes and behaviors also elicit certain expectancies and behaviors in teachers. In other words, students invite or disinvite teachers just as teachers invite or disinvite students. This process has been documented by Bellack, Kliebard, Hyman, and Smith (1966) and will be considered in greater detail in Chapter 4. But regardless of the presence or absence of invitations from students, teachers have the power and responsibility to invite all students consistently. The teacher who explains his or her lack of invitations to students by saying, "When students invite me, I'll invite them," is like a governor who says, "When we get better prisoners, we'll have better prisons." The teacher is the professional person in the relationship. He or she is, or should be, the primary source of invitations. Consistent invitations to learning, regardless of student apathy, remote administration, insensitive parents, dispirited colleagues, or "last year's teacher," lie within each teacher's power. It will be useful to examine teacher power more closely.

TEACHER POWER

The capacity to invite or disinvite, to determine who will be invited or disinvited and how, and to establish the "rules" under which invitations or disinvitations are extended, rests with the teacher. No matter how bad the school situation, the teacher never loses the power to invite or disinvite students. This is a power that teachers can control and be responsible for. Recognizing, accepting, and using this ability can be a tremendous advantage for teachers. "Yes, I remember a most definite invitation," a student wrote. "I was at my desk, and I was twisting a ring around my finger. My teacher must have noticed, because he said, 'Cynthia, I can tell you're nervous about something. May I help?' Well, I was so impressed because I thought he could read my mind. I also thought what a marvelous person to be so perceptive and to really know and care how I felt inside." The invitations of a single teacher may not always be sufficient, but they are always significant. If nothing more, his or her invitations will probably have a cumulative effect, increasing the likelihood that another teacher's invitations will be accepted at some future time.

The cumulative effect of experiences is an important principle of human development. As explained by Combs, Avila, and Purkey (1971, p. 59): "Life is not reversible; every experience a person has, he has had forever. One cannot unexperience what has happened to him. Any meaningful experience or series of experiences may not be sufficient to produce the changes we hope for. But they are always important." Any invitation that invites young people to be able, valuable, and responsible persons is not wasted. Each invitation, no matter how small or in what area, can potentially make a significant contribution to the student's sense of self-esteem— particularly if the invitation is accepted and successfully acted upon by the student.

Recognizing their power to send invitations and understanding the significance of each invitation provides teachers with confidence and strength in the face of apparent apathy, indifference, or even hostility. Whether a teacher's invitations are accepted or rejected, as we shall see in Chapter 4, depends on many factors that sometimes lie beyond the control of teachers, parents, or others. Behavior is determined by a lifetime of meanings that influence how students see themselves, others, and the world. The task of the teacher, therefore, is to extend the most suitable invitations to learning, to carefully note how these invitations appear in the eyes of students, and to respond accordingly with additional invitations.

Teachers should also understand that fundamental changes in students occur slowly. Sometimes teachers never see the final results of their efforts; the influence of an invitation may not be visible for weeks, months, or even years. Fortunately, invitations to see oneself in basically positive ways have the power to influence behavior long after they are extended. One college student wrote: "When I was in the fifth grade, I was very sick and almost died. My teacher called our home every day. Later when I returned to school, he helped me catch up. I'll always remember his kindness, and someday I hope to write a book which says: 'Dedicated to Mr. Norman Siegal'."

PATTERNS OF COMMUNICATION

The process of inviting students to learn is complex. A teacher's invitations are difficult to explain as a chain of events or as the contents of a message. Invitations to learning are often intangible and can be so subtle and indirect that teachers and students are sometimes unaware of their effects. A certain pattern exists, however, in the endless variety of messages transmitted in the school. By bringing this pattern into focus, we can identify teacher behaviors that result in students feeling powerfully *invited* or *disinvited* in their school careers. Let us consider these two feelings in turn.

The Invited

Over the past few years, more than 2,000 students at various grade levels have provided me examples of invitations or disinvitations they received during their time in school. The great majority of students clearly remembered what it was like to feel invited in school. Each of their illustrations fell into one of three basic categories: (1) invitations to be responsible.

(2) invitations to be capable, and (3) invitations to feel valuable. Students of various ages gave these examples:

INVITATIONS TO BE RESPONSIBLE

"Coach asked me to take the equipment out and explain the rules."

"She didn't try to force us to work, but she made it clear that we hurt ourselves by goofing off."

"When I decided to choose French over Spanish, I could tell that the Spanish teacher respected my decision."

"She let us do something on our own, she trusted us."

"I remember my third-grade teacher telling me how proud she was of our behavior during her absence—she said we were like sixth-graders!"

INVITATIONS TO BE CAPABLE

"Mr. Mac said I had made the most progress of anyone in the class."

"I remember my science teacher saying I was a careful researcher."

"My teacher asked me if she could take a copy of my paper to show at a teachers' workshop."

"She was enthusiastic about my poetry and arranged to have it entered in a contest."

"Coach said I had a natural ability if I had the desire."

"Mrs. Warren would write 'très bon' on our paper when she was pleased."

INVITATIONS TO FEEL VALUABLE

"Mr. Toppe cared enough to come to school a half hour early each morning just to help me with math."

"The teacher treated us like we were somebody. I recall the time she invited all of us to her home for a cookout."

"The first day of school my teacher said she was going to teach me how to smile; and she did!"

"Our teacher kept us in during a recess and taught us how to sit. All the girls felt like we were being invited to be ladies."

> **"I could tell the counselor was genuinely interested in me. She was willing to listen, and she responded with feeling."**

> **"Mrs. Smith encouraged us to like ourselves and to take pride in our work."**

Again and again, students reported that particular teachers in their lives had a flair for extending powerful invitations. One student wrote: "Whenever I was in Miss Penn's English class, I could *feel* myself becoming more intelligent!"

It is not surprising that students learn best when placed in the hands of teachers who invite them to see themselves as responsible, capable, and valuable. Unfortunately, many students describe memories of their schooling that center around feelings of being irresponsible, incapable, and worthless. When asked to describe the invitations they received in school, these students reported disinvitations.

The Disinvited

Many students reported that they felt disinvited in school simply because they were consistently overlooked. They said they were seldom encouraged to participate in school activities, that they rarely played on a team, belonged to a club, held an office, or attended a school function. They stated that they simply did not feel a part of school and that they seldom related with teachers in even the most casual personal way. Their teachers usually returned papers without comment, except for a letter grade, and rarely seemed to notice the students' absences from school. These students suffered from a "caring disability"; not enough teachers cared enough to invite them to participate.

A vivid portrait of a disinvited child is presented by Mizer (1964), who describes how schools can function to turn a child "into a zero." Mizer illustrates the tragedy of one such child, then concludes her article with these words (p. 10):

> I look up and down the rows carefully each September at the unfamiliar faces. I look for veiled eyes or bodies scrounged into a seat in an alien world. "Look, Kids," I say silently, "I may not do anything else for you this year, but not one of you is going to come out of here a nobody. I'll

work or fight to the bitter end doing battle with society and the school board, but I won't have one of you coming out of here thinking of himself as a zero."

Children need invitations the way flowers need sunshine. When they are treated with indifference, they are likely to become indifferent to themselves and to school. They begin to say to themselves, "Give up, no one cares about your small victories." This general process has been described by Willis (1970) as "systematic extinction." What it means for the teacher is that students who have learned to feel bad about themselves as learners are vulnerable to additional failure, just as a physically weak person is susceptible to illness.

Adding to the problem of indifferent treatment, students who continuously feel overlooked and disinvited may decide to seek revenge. Most students are acutely aware when some are given more opportunities and more encouragement than others. Those who are disinvited keenly remember the slights they receive. And one angry student bent on destruction can vandalize an entire school, just as one frustrated person with a rifle can redirect the course of human history.

In equally tragic shape are students who are not just ignored but are actively *dissuaded* from attending school. As one middle-school student wrote, "I really don't have enough time to tell how many times I've been disinvited in school." Much of this dissuasion can be traced to formal school policy. According to 1970 U.S. census data, two million children missed all or a substantial portion of their school year. The Children's Defense Fund Reports of School Suspensions (*Children Out of School in America,* 1975) concluded that these children were absent not simply by choice but because they were systematically excluded.

Since 1970, the use of suspensions as disciplinary actions in public schools has reached staggering proportions. In the 1972—73 school year, school districts enrolling over half the student population of the United States suspended one out of every twenty-four students. More striking, the suspension rate for black secondary school students was one out of eight! These figures do not include *de facto* suspensions, where students are suspended, never return, and are reported as "drop-outs" (*Children Out of School in America,* 1975).

Contrary to popular belief, the vast majority of school suspensions were for nonviolent offenses such as truancy, tardiness, pregnancy, smoking, violation of dress code, or failure to purchase required materials and equipment. While approximately one third of the suspensions involved fighting, all but a tiny fraction of these were for fights between students rather than for incidents of violence against faculty (*Children Out of School in America,* 1975). Fortunately, there is growing recognition that students have constitutional rights to attend school and to receive an education and that these rights cannot be denied without a formal review and due process considerations.

The problem of being educationally "disenfranchised" is compounded among lower socioeconomic groups, where students are sometimes more disinvited than disadvantaged. In his research on self-fulfilling prophecy in ghetto education, Rist (1970) concluded that teachers inadvertently stratify students in accordance with perceived social-class membership. This tends to perpetuate a "caste system," which reinforces group prejudices and antagonisms in many classrooms.

A second practice that can disinvite many children from achieving in school is that of labeling and grouping. While some classification is probably essential, educators are growing more concerned that the proliferation of new syndromes and the negative consequences of labeling and grouping may outweigh the intended benefits of meeting the academic needs of students who require special help (Borg, 1966; Findley and Bryan, 1975; Hobbs, 1975a, 1975b; Lederer, 1968; McGinley and McGinley, 1970; Rist, 1970; Schrank, 1968, 1970). As Hobbs (1975b) warns: "Categories and labels are powerful instruments for social regulation and control, and they often are employed for obscure, covert or hurtful purposes: to degrade people, to deny them access to opportunity, to exclude 'undesirables' whose presence in society in some way offends, disturbs familiar custom, or demands extraordinary efforts" (p. 10). Rist (1970) has also described this "locking in" process whereby untold numbers of children are labeled in their earliest days of schooling as retarded, learning-disabled, emotionally disturbed, hyperkinetic, brain-dysfunctioned, cognitively disordered, cognitively disadvantaged, maladjusted, or simply as "slow learners." These children are then sorted, separated, grouped, and treated differently than "normal" students. This differential treatment is likely to be perpetuated year after year, particularly when educators pay greater attention to the label than to the child.

A vivid example of how labels can disinvite is provided by Bogdan and Taylor (1976). A 26-year-old man who had been labeled "mentally retarded" told the researchers (Bogdan and Taylor, 1976, p. 48):

> The problem is getting labeled as being something. After that you're not really seen as a person. It's like a sty in your eye—it's noticeable. Like that teacher and the way she looked at me. In the fifth grade—in the fifth grade my classmates thought I was different, and my teacher knew I was different. One day she looked at me and she was on the phone in the room. I was there. She looked at me and knew I was knowledgeable about what she was saying. Her negative picture of me stood out like a sore thumb.

Institutional practices that diagnose "deviates" and bracket them in "modified programs" encourage both teachers and parents to expect certain levels of performance that may doom some children to educational inferiority. "In our school," one student commented, "the special class is a garbage disposal."

Research evidence on how labeling influences perceptions has been provided by Frericks (1974), who demonstrated the effects of telling prospective teachers that a classroom of students, viewed on videotape, was a class of "low-ability" students. A control group watched the same videotape but was told that it showed "regular students in a normal classroom." After watching the videotape, both groups of prospective teachers completed a scale designed to measure their attitudes toward the videotaped students. Compared to the control group, the experimental group of prospective teachers who had been told the students were "low ability" viewed them as less responsible, possessing less self-control, more prone to rudeness, and showing less capacity to engage in an abstract level of discussion. These findings agree with those of other studies, which indicate that labeling and grouping can carry a number of penalties. In reading, for example, some teachers tend to express negative feelings toward children of lower-skill reading groups (McGinley and McGinley, 1970; Stevens, 1971) and tend to have "inappropriately low expectations" for them (Brophy and Good, 1974, p. 81). One student described the stigmatizing process this way: "It's OK to be clumsy, and it's OK to be silly, but if you're both clumsy and silly, you're labeled a retard." For too many students, the school is a "high-risk neighborhood."

Evidence that labeling and grouping have the power to stigmatize students is increasing. As Findley and Bryan (1975) state: "Assignment to low achievement groups carries a stigma that is generally more debilitating than relatively poor achievement in heterogeneous groups" (p. 20). "When they put me in the bone-head class," one student wrote, "I wanted to walk out the door and never come back." In view of our present understanding of the disinviting qualities of labeling and ability grouping, it seems tragic that the practice continues to be so widespread.

There are positive signs, however, that labeling and ability grouping are abating. Certain efforts are being made to alter the processes that disinvite students and contribute to the problems of low achievement (Baroff, 1974; Frericks, 1974; Hobbs, 1975a, 1975b). Fresh approaches, such as mainstreaming, are being developed in order to avoid the labeling and isolating of students into pejorative environments. More sensitive and discriminating ways are beginning to focus on specific problems and behaviors of individual children. Throughout the helping professions, there is a growing awareness of the disinviting aspects of labeling and grouping.

Beyond the formal school policies of suspending, expelling, labeling, and grouping, many students are disinvited by teachers who, either intentionally or unintentionally, behave in ways that result in student embarrassment, frustration, and failure. "My Latin teacher did not like females, particularly 'socially oriented' ones," a high-school girl wrote. "And I met both requirements. I was in a room with my best friends, which included males and females. The teacher would pick me out and have me go to the board and write something in Latin. Of course, when I missed something, which was often, the entire class got a lecture on studying more and socializing less. But I had to stand in front of the class by myself the entire time while the lecture on the evils of 'socializing' was being presented. I was usually so embarrassed I would end up crying in the bathroom where no one could see me."

Canfield and Wells (1976) use the term "killer statements" to describe the means by which a student's feelings, thoughts, and creative behaviors are "killed off" by another person's negative comments, physical gestures, or other behavior. These actions may be little more than a teacher's suddenly stiffened spine when a child of another race touches his or her shoulder—or as elusive as a teacher who seldom calls on certain children in the classroom.

A child's feelings of being disinvited are described by Dick Gregory in his autobiography *Nigger* (1964): "The teacher thought I was a troublemaker. All she saw from the front of the room was a little black boy who squirmed in his idiot's seat and made noises and poked the kids around him. I guess she couldn't see a kid who made noises because he wanted someone to know he was there" (p. 30). People have profound influence on each other, and whether intentionally or unintentionally, a teacher's inviting or disinviting behavior can have profound effects on students.

Students who reported that they felt disinvited in school described experiences that fall into three categories: (1) feelings of being irresponsible, (2) feelings of being incapable, and (3) feelings of being worthless. Here are some samples of how these feelings were elicited:

FEELINGS OF BEING IRRESPONSIBLE

"The teacher said I didn't want to learn, that I just wanted to cause trouble."

"She said I was worse than my brother, and I don't even have a brother."

"Because I failed to bring my homework, the counselor asked me why I bothered coming to school."

"She told the class we were discipline problems and were not to be trusted."

"The teacher put me out in the hall for everyone to laugh at."

FEELINGS OF BEING INCAPABLE

"They put me in the dummy class, and it had SPECIAL EDUCATION painted right on the door."

"The teacher said to me in front of the whole class: 'I really don't think you're that stupid.'"

"When the principal hit me, he said it was the only language I understood."

"They kept telling me I got to learn to keep my mouth shut and stay in my seat."

"I was asked if I had enough sense to follow simple directions."

FEELINGS OF BEING WORTHLESS

"On the first day of school, the teacher came in and said he wasn't supposed to teach this basic class, but that he was stuck with us."

"My name is Bill Dill, but the teacher always called me 'Dill Pickle' and laughed."

"The teacher said 'That's crazy! What's the matter with you?' His negative attitude toward me stood out like a bump on your nose."

"I transferred to a new school after it had started. When I appeared at the teacher's doorway, she said 'Oh, no, not another one!'"

Of course, negative experiences may spur someone to future success, but this will likely be true only of students who do not easily accept rejection and failure. Students who fight back against disinvitations do so only because they have a past history of invitations received, accepted, and successfully acted upon. They have built up a partial immunity to failure. Students who readily accept disinvitations are usually those who have been infected with failure early in life. As one student wrote: "Hell, how can I feel good about myself when I'm stuck in the dummy class year after year?"

The explicit picture drawn from countless descriptions is that students live in a world of attitudes, expectancies, and evaluations received from the school environment. While the full impact of these messages has yet to be determined, it seems clear that student success or failure is related to the ways in which students perceive themselves and the world—and that these perceptions are influenced by the prevailing nature of the invitations or disinvitations extended to them by significant others.

WHY INVITATIONS ARE IMPORTANT

Everything the teacher does, as well as the manner in which he does it, incites the child to respond in some way or another and each response tends to set the child's attitude in some way or another.

John Dewey *How We Think*
(1933, p. 59)

Current research evidence is scarce, but it can be hypothesized that individuals have a basic need to be noticed, and noticed favorably, by others. As William James (1890) commented long ago: "No more fiendish punishment could be devised, were such a thing possible, than that one should be turned loose in society and remain absolutely unnoticed by all the members thereof" (p. 179). This same basic human need was described by Martin Buber: "Man wishes to be confirmed in his being by man, and wishes to have a presence in the being of the other. . . . secretly and bashfully he watches for a Yes which allows him to be and which can come only from one human person to another. It is from one person to another that the heavenly bread of self-being is passed" (1965, p. 71).

If you have ever jumped from a bathtub to answer a ringing phone or groped in a mailbox at 3:00 A.M. after arriving home from a long trip, you can vouch for the pulling power of a potential invitation. Invitations are almost always welcome, even if they come from someone other than a best friend. Teaching machines and programed materials have an important place in education, but they are poor substitutes for an inviting human relationship. As Jourard (1968) has indicated, teaching is a way of being with people. It is this "being-with" process that is most likely to have the greatest impact on students' ideas about themselves and their abilities. Even more than being-with, the concept of an invitation suggests a *bidding* to be somewhere, to look ahead to tomorrow's joy and fulfillment, to have something to live *for* and look forward *to*. As we've seen, invitational teachers *see* something in students that students may not *see* in themselves, and they invite students to share in these perceptions.

Most teachers who have taught for awhile understand that students have a basic need for self-regard and regard from others. This need was described by an elementary-school teacher who wrote: "Recently, in my second-grade class, I had each child express what he or she would like to be as an adult. After listening to each child, I said: 'Everybody look up at your star in the sky and reach for it!' Every child in the room started reaching as high as possible. The amazing thing is that they all want to do something good each day just so I can say to them: 'Reach up and see if you're a little bit closer to your star.'" Each human watches closely for clues in the behavior of others; a teacher's words, winks, smiles, nods, or touches can be marvelously reassuring to a child struggling with a difficult spelling word, a complex math problem, a threatening oral report, or an effort to reach a star.

FOUR LEVELS OF TEACHING

When you and I considered the power of teachers to extend invitations, we learned that the person extending the invitation always has the power to determine the "rules" under which the invitation is extended. In this sense, invitations are always intentional. On the other hand, it is possible for a person to be *un*intentionally inviting or disinviting, for what is inviting or disinviting remains in the eyes of the beholder. The best-intentioned actions of a teacher may not be viewed positively by students—just as a student's invitation may be viewed negatively by teachers.

Many problems in the school result from communications that are misconceived, misdirected, or misunderstood. For instance, a teacher's invitation to students to play "drop the handkerchief" may appeal to a first-grade class, but will probably be very disinviting to sixth-graders. Thus, teachers usually function at one of four apparent levels: *Level 1: intentionally disinviting; Level 2: unintentionally disinviting; Level 3: unintentionally inviting;* and *Level 4: intentionally inviting.* While all teachers function at all levels from time to time, most teachers appear to function typically at one level more than others. It will be helpful to consider these four levels more closely.

Level 1: Intentionally Disinviting
It is painful to acknowledge that a few teachers spend a significant part of

their time intentionally disinviting students. Yet, based on numerous reports from students of various ages, there are teachers and other school personnel who spend considerable time informing students that they are incapable, worthless, and irresponsible. One student wrote: "When I first attended an integrated school, a teacher looked at me, then turned to another teacher and said: 'Some children do not belong in this school.'" A second student wrote: "The teacher was against me no matter what I did." And a third student reported that she was advised not to go to college because her intelligence-test scores were too low. Whether because of racial prejudice, unrequited love, personal inadequacy, sadistic impulse, or negative self-image, certain people in the helping professions function at the *intentionally disinviting* level. These people themselves might benefit from professional help. If they are unable or unwilling to accept help, the apparent duty of fellow professionals is to remove them from daily contact with students. Fortunately, relatively few teachers and other school workers function at the *intentionally disinviting* level.

Level 2: Unintentionally Disinviting

A much larger problem in schools is the unintentionally disinviting teacher. Such teachers are usually well-meaning and high-minded, but their teaching methods belie their good intentions. Their teaching is usually characterized by boredom, "busy work," and insensitivity to feelings. Examples of such insensitivity appear again and again in student accounts of being disinvited: "I feel insulted when faculty sponsors always ask a female to take minutes," wrote one girl. Another student described how she was disinvited by a teacher who said: "You're invited to try out for the part . . . if you really want to." A third student expressed her frustration over a teacher who always referred to her as "Negro" rather than "black." Teacher behavior perceived by students as chauvinistic, condescending, or patronizing is likely to be interpreted as a disinvitation regardless of the teacher's intention.

As mentioned earlier, the primary source of students' feeling disinvited is probably the tendency of teachers to focus on certain groups as being "different." By talking at length about "learning disabilities," "culturally disadvantaged," or "emotionally disturbed," the concept of "being different" may unintentionally encourage feelings of inferiority in students. This self-fulfilling circle is closed when those so labeled accept the label and begin to behave accordingly.

Level 3: Unintentionally Inviting

Just as it is possible to be friendly without being a friend, so it is possible to be inviting without sending an invitation. To illustrate, one first-grade teacher has the habit of squatting down when she talks to young children so that she can approach them at their eye level. One day this teacher squatted down to chat with a group of kindergarteners; suddenly, as if by magic, the children squatted down too. Her behavior was interpreted by the children as an invitation to squat!

Probably many so-called "natural-born teachers," those who have never taken a professional education course but who are highly effective in the classroom, are successful because they are unintentionally inviting. They typically behave in ways that result in student feelings of being invited, although they remain unaware of the dynamics involved. The problem in functioning at the unintentionally inviting level is that the teacher is not in a position to identify the causes of his or her successes or failures. If whatever "it" is should stop working, the teacher does not know how to start it up again or what changes to make in his or her behavior. We do not *know* what we are doing until we can *identify* what we are doing. For this reason, the best way to invite school success is to be intentionally inviting.

Level 4: Intentionally Inviting

From the point of view presented here, teachers should try to be intentionally inviting. The more explicit an invitation, the more it lends itself to evaluation, direction, and modification. "Miss Penn always used our *real* names when speaking to us," one student wrote. "Other teachers might call you 'honey' or 'sweetheart,' but Miss Penn always called us by our real names. She told us at the beginning of the year that she had difficulty in remembering names, so if she called us by the wrong name, not to get upset. She said that when she used a real name, even if it was the wrong one, it showed us that she was trying to learn each student's name. We appreciated that."

Being explicit about the invitations we send to students helps us check the accuracy of our perceptions and avoid the problems of misunderstanding that appear in many schools.

Recognition of the power to be intentionally inviting and the use of this power can be tremendous assets for teachers and other professionals in education. By understanding the four levels of teaching and working to operate at the intentionally inviting level (at least most of the time), teachers can be a significant force in inviting school success.

In this opening chapter, we have seen that some students are powerfully invited to learning, some are overlooked, and some are told to stay away. We have reviewed evidence that individuals respond best when they share the company of teachers who believe them to be valuable, capable, and responsible, and who invite them to realize their abilities. Chapter 2 will present the significance of self-concept in inviting school success.

concerns. When I had finished, he said, 'I won't tell you you *should* go to college, but I can tell you you are *capable* enough to go.'" The student described this counselor as follows: "He always had time to listen to our complaints. . . . Maybe he really couldn't change a thing, but at least he cared to listen."

A major aspect of caring to listen is to listen with care. Listening with care is the process whereby the teacher attends carefully to students in order to understand how his or her invitations to learning are being received, interpreted, and acted upon. This general process has been called *reflective listening* (Canfield and Wells, 1976), *active listening* (Gordon, 1974), *resonating with the client* (Rogers, 1951), and *attending* (Egan, 1975). Perhaps blinded Gloucester in Shakespeare's *King Lear* described the process best when he said, "I see it feelingly" (act 4, scene 6). But whatever term we use, we are talking about the process whereby teachers work to understand what is occurring inside the perceptual world of the student. This calls for "reading behavior backwards"—for looking beyond the student's overt behavior to infer what that behavior indicates about the student's internal world. A student's bitter complaint of helplessness over an assigned problem, for example, may mean that the student is feeling frustration and is asking for reassurance. This skill of reading behavior backwards is so important that Richards and Richards (1975) postulated that the training of teachers who can understand how things seem from another person's viewpoint should be a major goal of teacher education programs.

In the final analysis, the individual is the world's greatest authority on that individual. Only the person with the pain knows where it hurts. For teachers this means that their invitations are invariably perceived by students in the light of the students' past experiences. This process has been documented by Dowaliby and Schumer (1973), Felker (1974), and others, who have shown that individual students in the classroom perceive differently what happens to them. To be asked to wash the blackboard may be viewed as an invitation by one child, but as a definite disinvitation by another. No two individuals ever share exactly the same past, and no two students ever perceive a teacher's invitation in the same way. If we are to understand why an invitation to learning is or is not accepted by a student, we must first listen to understand how that invitation appears and sounds in the eyes and ears of the beholder. Here is an example of how things appear differently when seen from an internal point of view: "Some years ago I had a high-school student who appeared to be very poised and self-confident and who played the guitar with marvelous skill," wrote a teacher. "Yet we could never get him to accept our invitation to perform in public. Other teachers said it was because he felt superior to others in the school. But one day he confided in me that he would dearly love to perform, but stage fright made him physically sick with fear."

Listening with care is also important because students sometimes do not know how to—or cannot—respond appropriately to a teacher's invitations. Often students would *like* to accept an invitation to learning, but for personal reasons feel unable to do so. Because of self-doubt ("How could I ever learn this stuff?"), threat ("I'm afraid I'll look stupid if I try"), hostility ("They just want to make fun of me"), or resignation ("I know I can't do math"), many students have difficulty in responding to even the most attractive invitations. As William James (1890) reminded us: "To give up pretensions is as blessed a relief as to get them gratified, and where disappointment is incessant and the struggle unending, that is what men always do" (pp. 310—311).

As mentioned earlier, students with special problems are likely to perceive the teacher's invitations in unusual ways. The same encouragement may have sharply different meanings to different children, even children of the same age. The shy, insecure child may experience great anxiety at a teacher's invitation to read a story in front of the class. A child with high self-assurance may find the same invitation most attractive. Also, children with severe behavioral difficulties or children filled with feelings of anger and frustration may find acceptance of the most well-meaning invitations from teachers or peers very difficult. One teacher described such a student this way: "Tracy comes to school each day with hands clenched tightly, face in a frown. Nothing ever seems to go right for him. The least thing a child does to him will definitely end in a fight. His peers are always cheating him when playing games. The teacher has never liked him. The work is too hard. He leaves school each day with hands clenched tightly, face in a frown."

Children such as Tracy are likely to hide their true feelings, and a teacher's invitations to feel able, valuable, and responsible may appear to be the last things they want. But invitational teachers are not misled. They understand that students who hold negative feelings about themselves face a great risk when they accept a teacher's invitations, for they become vulnerable to further hurt. They also understand that, for students who have been consistently disinvited, a handful of invitations are seldom enough to make an observable difference in behavior. Invitational teachers recognize the problems involved yet continue to believe their efforts worthwhile. They recognize that students must be invited consistently, and so they persevere and invite again and again and again, filling the classroom with invitations.

Finally, listening with care means that the teacher is alert for the faintest signal from students that might indicate their desire to respond to an invitation: clearing of a throat, leaning forward, hand half-raised, eye contact, lingering after class. Invitational teachers are aware of such positive nonverbal signals and take special responsibility for encouraging acceptance of invitations. They are also responsible for doing everything possible to ensure that students who accept invitations to learning have a good chance of success, for they understand that failure after the risk of accepting an invitation can have long-lasting effects. A graduate student described teacher efforts to maximize chances of student success this way: "An invitational teacher is like a good quarterback in football. When the quarterback throws a pass to a moving receiver, he tries to hit the receiver in full stride and maximize his motion, to get into the flow of energy of the receiver and to move with him instead of trying to redirect him." By listening for clues in the variations of student behavior, invitational teachers are able to "get into the flow" of student energy so that the chances of misunderstanding are minimized and the chances of success are maximized.

BEING REAL WITH STUDENTS

Carl Rogers has given some valuable suggestions on ways to invite students to learn (1965, 1967, 1971, 1976). Along with "prizing" the learner and empathic understanding of the learner's point of view, Rogers has emphasized the importance of genuineness ("realness") in the teacher's relationships with students. This quality was described by a high-school student who wrote: "My best teacher was great because she was real and not a phony. She expressed her feelings like a human being." It can also help to share some home experiences with students, letting them know that their teacher is a fellow human being who burns the toast, washes the car, and loses the house key just like everyone else. A basic quality of the invitational teacher is to be "real," to be able to face students without phoniness or a false front.

For the invitational teacher, the concept of realness requires that any invitation extended to students should be credible. Praise, for example, should be based on honest performance. While praise generally produces increases in effort (Bavelas, Hastorf, Gross, and Kite, 1965; Cantrell, Wood, and Nichols, 1974; Costello, 1964), compliments tossed out to students with little or no justification quickly lose all meaning. One student referred to his teacher as a "dead cat teacher"—"if you brought her a dead cat, she would praise it." Researching the dangers of excessive praise shows that many young people simply "tune out" the frequent verbal praise of adults (Brophy and Evertson, 1976), a result probably due to the unrealistic amount of praise distributed by some teachers, parents, and friends.

The importance of realistic praise has been demonstrated by Rowe (1974a), who found that students ranked "poorest" by teachers actually received *more* verbal praise than those ranked "best." It was difficult, however, to determine what the bottom students were being praised for; as much as 50 percent of the praise did not appear attached to correct responding. Rowe commented that bottom students "generally receive an ambiguous signal system" (1974c, p. 298). In other words, what these students did or did not do seemed unrelated to the praise they received. In comparison, top students received *less* verbal praise, but the praise they did receive was more pertinent to their responses. What Rowe's research means for teachers is that actions taken to encourage academic achievement and self-regard must be realistic and relevant to honest performance. As an example, the teacher might say, "Bill, you've covered a lot of territory today. You've learned the process of carrying numbers. I'm very pleased with your progress."

Realness in the teacher does not, of course, rely simply on the presence or absence of praise or other verbal messages. We communicate with our entire bodies. Many researchers have provided ample evidence that we constantly communicate our real feelings with the language of behavior (Argyle, 1975; Gazda, 1973; Hall, 1959; Hennings, 1974; Insel and Jacobson, 1975; Mehrabian, 1971, 1972). With every verbal message (for example, "Welcome to the fifth grade"), there is also the behavioral message. The nonverbal message may lie in the teacher's tone of voice, physical appearance, body stance, facial expression, gestures, and physical proximity. Eye contact especially—looking directly at a particular student—can signal, "I am sincere in what I say, and my welcome is aimed directly at you." A warm tone of voice, a neat physical appearance, a friendly smile, and direct eye contact all communicate that the student really is welcome to the fifth grade. On the other hand, a teacher's aloof behavior, forced smile, tightly crossed arms, or indifferent manner may say more clearly than words, "I would rather not be here with you." Nonverbal language is so important that a hallmark of invitational teaching is to ensure that eye contact, body posture, facial expression, and voice tone agree with the teacher's verbal messages. For example, invitational teachers look serious when stating displeasure; they look at a student when expressing sincerity; and they tense their bodies when expressing frustration. Their body language agrees with their spoken language.

Because students are quick to spot conflicts between what teachers say and how they behave, it is vital for invitational teachers, in Kraft's (1975) words, to "come on straight." Coming on straight means sharing feelings of happiness, anger, enthusiasm, sadness, excitement, or boredom. Teachers able to express their true feelings are more likely to be seen as "real" by students. One high-school student expressed the importance of "real" behavior in a teacher with these words: "I remember that our high-school history teacher was not afraid to express his feelings. He let us know when our misbehavior was getting to him. But he didn't show just his angry side. Once he cried at the end of a movie shown in class when the hero died. I learned a lot from him besides history . . . that it's OK for a man to express an emotion besides anger."

Coming on straight does not mean unbridled self-disclosure. While obvious advantages are involved in self-disclosure and sharing one's feelings with others, such sharing should not be overdone. Disclosure, as Derlega and Chaikin (1975) emphasize, should be appropriate to the situation. If others casually ask us how we are, for example, they usually do not expect a complete medical history.

The choice of self-disclosure is also determined by how comfortable one feels in revealing oneself to others. We vary in how much we choose to share. Some teachers are more "open" than others. It is important, therefore, that teachers take their own feelings into account when determining how much of themselves they choose to share with other people.

Perhaps the best way to summarize the importance of being real with students is to quote the words of a classroom teacher: "During the real 'up tight' period of the school year following Christmas vacation, I found a note under my classroom door. It read: 'Mr. Maggor, be yourself, don't try to be someone you're not.' It was signed 'A student and a friend.' Suddenly I realized that I had been coming down hard and mean on little things, which was not me and not my usual behavior. Later the two students, neither of whom I had in class, stopped by and talked with me about it. That day I learned a lot about the importance of being myself with my students." It is fortunate that teachers are not the only ones capable of being real and that many teachers will accept invitations as well as send them.

BEING REAL WITH ONESELF

Being real with students is much easier when teachers have a positive, realistic view of themselves. A growing body of literature in the fields of education and psychology centers on the assumption that when teachers better understand and accept themselves, they have a much greater capacity to accept and understand students (Combs, Avila, and Purkey, 1971, 1978; Jersild, 1952, 1965; Patterson, 1973; Rogers, 1951; 1967). Researchers have reported significant relationships between teacher self-regard and such factors as how they evaluate students (Drugger, 1971), how effective they tend to be as teachers (Usher and Hanke, 1971), how students see themselves (Landry, 1974), and how well students achieve on standardized tests (Aspy and Buhler, 1975). Emerging evidence indicates that a positive, realistic view of oneself is an important ingredient in becoming an invitational teacher. "Mrs. Reynolds expected good things of us," a high-school student wrote, "and we could tell she also expected good things of herself."

Being real with oneself as a teacher is particularly important when working with students from backgrounds different from one's own background. Braun (1976) has emphasized that one of the most important things that teachers can do in the classroom is become aware of their own biases and stereotypes toward certain students and recognize the influence of these perceptions on the academic performance of students. Teachers who claim to be "objective" in dealing with students are probably deluding themselves, for it is highly unlikely that any human being can be "objective" about anything of any consequence. At the same time, one *may* recognize one's own prejudices and biases and take them into account when dealing with students of varying backgrounds. Teachers who continuously boast that "some of my best friends are of another race" are perhaps being less than honest with themselves about their attitudes. Fair play in the classroom can be accomplished only when teachers are honest with themselves about their own feelings.

Being honest with oneself does not demand self-depreciation and destructive self-criticism. On the contrary, the ability to speak *to* oneself *about* oneself in positive, realistic ways is an important quality of invitational teaching. To understand this, imagine two science teachers. Both possess essentially the same knowledge and skills. During each teacher's class, two students carry on a private conversation, ignoring the carefully prepared demonstration by the teacher. This student behavior elicits different internal dialogues (what we say to ourselves about ourselves) from the two teachers.

The first teacher thinks to himself: "I've stayed up half the night to prepare this demonstration, and those two students are not paying a bit of attention to me. I know I'm not the greatest teacher, but why do kids have to be so rude?"

The second teacher, faced with exactly the same student behavior, is more realistic and thinks something like this: "Those two students are not paying attention. That's too bad, because this is an important and well-prepared demonstration. I'll try to find additional ways to make these demonstrations more interesting. Meanwhile, after class I'll tell them that their lack of attention is disturbing me."

The first teacher's internal dialogue is unrealistic and self-defeating. It exaggerates the meaning of the students' behavior; it emphasizes their lack of attention over the attention of all the other students in the class; and it overgeneralizes the situation by assuming personal inadequacy. Clearly, the first teacher's internal dialogue is inappropriate, anxiety-producing, and self-defeating. The second teacher makes a more positive appraisal of the classroom situation and forms a more realistic pattern of self-statements.

Awareness of one's internal dialogue and realistic appraisals of classroom experiences have been advocated by numerous researchers who report that what people say internally about themselves plays an important role in their adaptive or maladaptive behavior (Beck, 1970; Ellis, 1961; Lazarus and Averill, 1972; Meichenbaum, 1974; Meichenbaum, Gilmore, and Fedoravicius, 1971; Rimm and Litvak, 1969; Trexler and Karst, 1972; Veltin, 1968). In Mahoney's words, we need to "clean up what we say about ourselves" (1975, p. 865). Teachers are too often overly critical in what they say to themselves about themselves. "The worst enemies of teachers are teachers!" as one teacher noted. An important way to become an invitational teacher, therefore, is to be gentle with oneself and to practice a pattern of positive, realistic self-statements.

INVITING GOOD DISCIPLINE

Maintaining good discipline has been, and probably always will be, a major concern in education. Students tend to resist external control because it restricts personal choice and limits freedom. This love of individual freedom is a valuable part of the democratic ethic and should be cultivated rather than condemned. At the same time, teachers are responsible for maintaining reasonable control in the classroom and for achieving the goals set forth by society. To maintain order (usually called "discipline"), teachers have tried just about everything.

Earlier methods of discipline were essentially negative, and fear and punishment played dominant roles. One of the first schoolhouses built in the United States had a whipping post (Manning, 1959), and in the "good old

days" many techniques were devised to inflict physical punishment on er-
ring students. Fear, too, played a major role in maintaining discipline, and
children received ominous warnings from home, school, and the pulpit that
"the gobble-uns'll git you ef you don't watch out!" (James Whitcomb Riley,
"Little Orphant Annie").

Fortunately, more modern methods of maintaining classroom discipline
are generally positive. Dollar (1972), Dreikurs and Cassel (1974), Holmes,
Holmes, and Field (1974), Purkey and Avila (1971), Sloane (1976),
Williams and Kamala (1973), and others have provided some practical,
humane tips on how to deal with misbehavior. Behavior modification techniques, which attempt to reinforce desirable behavior and extinguish unde-
sirable behavior, are often effective. For behavior modification, the classroom is usually arranged so that when students behave in desirable ways,
desirable things happen to them. Reinforcement of this sort relies primarily
on rewards rather than punishments to modify and shape student behavior.
It should be noted, however, that both earlier and contemporary approaches treat discipline, whether rewarding or punishing, as primarily a
matter of employing certain techniques. Invitational teaching, by comparison, focuses on the teacher's belief system—that students are valuable, can
learn, and are responsible for their conduct. The teacher communicates
these beliefs within a framework of gentle but firm expectations for each
student.

Perhaps the most important belief of teachers relates to the dignity of
students. Whether intentionally or unintentionally, teachers and other professionals sometimes run roughshod over the personal feelings of students.
"My last name is Turley," a student wrote, "and my science teacher always
called me 'Turkey' and laughed. At first I felt hurt, and now I'm just resentful." When teachers employ tasteless humor, ridicule, and lack of respect
with students, it is not surprising that students reply in kind. Students are
likely to do unto teachers as teachers do unto them. In practical terms, this
means that teachers should practice common courtesy. Students who are
consistently treated with dignity and respect are less likely to cause problems
in the classroom. Conversely, students who think that teachers are out to
embarrass them and that the system is geared to convince them that they

are worthless, unable, and irresponsible will find ways to rebel, disrupt, and seek revenge—as humans have always done in their discontent and resentment. This is powerfully illustrated by the words of Shakespeare's hunchback Richard, "And therefore, since I cannot prove a lover to entertain these fair well-spoken days, I am determined to prove a villain!" (*Richard III,* act 1, scene 1). When students feel disinvited, they are unlikely to cooperate in the education process.

Beyond manifesting respect for students, good discipline is invited by teachers who believe that teaching should be as interesting as possible. When teachers recognize boredom as disinviting, they are more likely to seek ways to make their teaching as relevant and exciting as possible. Discipline problems diminish when students are interested and involved.

Finally, the ability to invite good discipline depends on the teacher's beliefs about what constitutes misbehavior. These beliefs vary considerably from teacher to teacher, school to school, and year to year. In 1848, for example, a North Carolina high school listed boys and girls playing together, girls wearing long fingernails, and boys neglecting to bow before going home as misbehaviors! Today most educators agree that rules should be reasonable, enforceable, and educationally relevant. Too often in the past, teachers and principals attempted to enforce rules that were ruthlessly authoritarian, generally disinviting, and—like regulations against tight pants, short skirts, long hair, and jewelry—had little relevance to education. With fewer and more reasonable rules, obviously, fewer rules are likely to be broken.

By now you may be thinking, "I believe these things about discipline, but some students still insist on causing disruption." This is true; students are not robots. Some will always resist control and discipline problems will always exist, even in the most inviting school environment. When misbehavior exceeds the reasonable limits established by the school, teachers and other school personnel might ask themselves: "What is happening here? Is the student upset or ill? Are certain factors in the school, such as temperature, class size, or time of day, eliciting misbehavior? How do students view themselves and others in the school? Does the student need professional counseling or other psychological help?" When satisfactory answers to questions like these do not excuse the misbehavior, a penalty is necessary. But even then, what the teacher believes about penalties makes a great difference. If teachers believe that penalties should be humane and used sparingly, they will resort to temporary denial of student privileges rather than to corporal punishment or psychological warfare. The important thing to remember about punishment is that it is the behavior that is unacceptable, not the student. Punishment should not give students the feeling of being disinvited or wronged and resentful. As A. S. Makarenko explained, the object of a penalty is to encourage the student to reflect on the offense, recognize why it was inappropriate, and take appropriate steps to correct it (Levin, 1959, p. 64).

Much has been written about maintaining discipline in the classroom, but little about ways to invite good discipline. For too long we have exonerated the disinviting behavior of some teachers by simply labeling students as "discipline problems." Perhaps now is the time to consider the reasons for misbehavior and to recognize that "an ounce of prevention is worth a pound of cure."

Because an invitational approach recognizes the limits of one's power to control others, particularly in maintaining classroom discipline, it will be helpful for us to consider ways in which teachers might handle student rejection of invitations.

HANDLING REJECTION

Today the majority of teachers are well trained, enthusiastic, and fired with hopes and ambitions for their students. Most teachers find their careers satisfying. They teach in schools filled with invitations, with zest for learning and respect for feelings. Other teachers, however, find themselves in less fortunate situations, swamped with assignments that appear to have little relevance to education. These nonteaching responsibilities include keeping monthly registers, floating schedules, and daily attendance records, as well as locker checks, hall monitoring, playground duty, lunchroom patrol—and a host of other nonteaching assignments. Teachers could more easily accept such duties if the duties were not coupled with overcrowded classes, dilapidated facilities, apparently bored and apathetic colleagues, and—perhaps most painful—disinterested and even hostile students who seem to reject the most well-intentioned invitations.

Faced with numerous rejections, the teacher can easily become disillusioned, bitter, and dejected, beginning to think: "Why should I continue to invite students? My invitations are not accepted. Besides, they're not in the union contract." When this thinking takes over, another potentially great teacher joins the ranks of teachers living a professional half-life. This loss of spirit and idealism is a terrible blow to education as well as a major calamity for the teacher. Such tragedy need not happen. When teachers operate with patience and courage, conserving and focusing limited energies at the most effective times, they will not be intimidated and overwhelmed by apparently impossible situations in which their finest invitations are rejected.

It is important, first, for teachers to determine whether or not their invitations are, in fact, being rejected by students. An apparent rejection of an invitation is often just the opposite. For example, one beginning teacher invited a student to help her move some supplies after class. "Are you jiving?" the student responded. "I got more important things to do." The teacher was resentful because she assumed that her invitation had been rudely rejected. Later she was startled when the student showed up to help. Minority-group members, especially, will accept or reject invitations in their own ways and on their own terms. It is important to understand that acceptances come in many forms. Just as the person who extends an invitation determines the "rules" under which it is extended, the person receiving the invitation determines how it will be acted upon.

Even when an invitation is definitely rejected, it is useful to separate one's invitation from oneself. Just because a student rejects an invitation does not mean that the student is rejecting the teacher. Students, like all of us, are not so much against others as *for* themselves. This endless quest for self-esteem was explained in Chapter 2. Because of the nature of self-concept, students may reject or accept invitations for countless reasons that have nothing to do with the teacher. One of the most common reasons for rejection of an invitation is the memory of similar invitations accepted in the past but found less than satisfying. If past invitations have hurt or humiliated us, it is a personal risk for us to accept present ones. Teachers who understand this process are less likely to blame themselves or consider it a personal insult when their invitations are rejected.

Beyond the psychological reasons for the rejection of invitations are environmental reasons as well. The physical conditions of teaching—room assignment, facilities, lighting, class size, temperature, general aesthetics, scheduling, even the class makeup of students with varying backgrounds and levels of achievement—all contribute to the acceptance or rejection of teacher invitations.

For those of us in teaching this means that we should work to avoid taking the rejection of an invitation personally. Students took a long time to arrive at where they are today, and they will also require time to change. Nevertheless, it is important to remember that everything makes a difference. Any invitation, no matter how small or in what area, has tremendous potential. As James Thomson wrote ("The Seasons," 1730):

> Oft, what seems
> A trifle, a mere nothing, by itself,
> In some nice situations, turns the scale
> Of fate, and rules the most important actions.

Even when we bake a loaf of bread, we have changed the world. And if we change the world by baking a loaf of bread, what marvelous opportunities we have in the classroom!

INVITING ONESELF

Peanuts © 1977 United Feature Syndicate, Inc.

The focus of this book does not lend itself to a detailed discussion of the many ways in which teachers may invite positive, realistic views of themselves. Many available books explore self-concept in detail and offer specific suggestions in this regard. Such books include those by Brophy and Evertson (1976); Bugental (1965); Combs, Avila, and Purkey (1971, 1978); Gardner (1965); Harris (1970); Jourard (1964, 1968); Moustakas (1966); Newman and Berkowitz (1971); Rogers (1951); and others. Many teachers also find in-service workshops, short courses, institutes, and other group participation activities useful in developing positive, realistic self-concepts.

Inviting oneself to realize one's own untapped potential is a tremendously important enterprise for teachers. As an old mountaineer once commented, "You can't come back from somewhere you ain't been." It is difficult to invite others if we have never invited ourselves. "The single relationship truly central and crucial in a life," stated Coudert (1965), "is the relationship to the self. It is rewarding to find someone whom you like, but it is essential to like yourself. It is quickening to recognize that someone is a good and decent human being, but it is indispensable to view yourself as acceptable. It is a delight to discover people who are worthy of admiration and respect and love, but it is vital to believe yourself deserving of these things" (p. 118). If we believe that invitations are important, then we begin with self-invitations: to stand tall, dress better, eat less, take exercise, become involved, join groups, and find ways to be present in this world.

It is helpful to keep in mind that the principles most useful for inviting others also apply in inviting oneself. Perhaps the most important principle is respect for oneself and one's feelings. Feelings are important, and to deny them is to deny one's existence. We are most likely to accept our own invitations when we take our feelings into account. For example, if exercising at night after a hard day of teaching feels terribly difficult, the teacher might try a self-invitation to exercise in the morning. If this doesn't work, a self-invitation to play a sport, buy an exercise bicycle, or take a long walk each evening might. The purpose is to send self-invitations that are most likely to be accepted and acted upon. By listening to our own feelings and varying our self-invitations, we increase the probability of success.

In this chapter, we've considered seven important skills of invitational teaching: reaching each student, listening with care, being real with students, being real with oneself, inviting good discipline, handling rejection, and inviting oneself. Examples of each skill were reviewed. The next chapter will present four factors that apparently relate to student self-concept as learner: (1) relating, (2) asserting, (3) investing, and (4) coping. These factors will be used to suggest concrete ways in which teachers may invite students to feel good about themselves as learners and to learn the course content.

5   *A KEY APPROACH*
TO INVITING

The used key is always bright.

Benjamin Franklin *Poor Richard's Almanac*
(1744)

Chapter 2 reviewed evidence indicating a significant relationship between self-concept and school achievement. On the basis of this evidence, we can see that students' perceptions of themselves *as learners* apparently serve as personal guidance systems to direct their classroom behavior. Assuming that self-concept as learner plays a critical part in students' academic performance, then a professional understanding of self-concept theory, coupled with skills for inferring how students view themselves as learners, are important tools for the invitational teacher.

This chapter is based on research provided by the *Florida Key* (Purkey, Cage, and Graves, 1973), an inventory of student behaviors designed to infer student self-concept as learner. The Key has been used since 1972 to investigate various groups of students, comparing disadvantaged and non-disadvantaged pupils (Owen, 1972), professed and inferred self-concepts of students (Graves, 1972), and students identified as disruptive and nondisruptive (Branch, 1974).

In making inferences about self-concept, most researchers have focused on *global* self-concept rather than on *situation-specific* self-images, such as self as athlete, self as family member, self as learner, or self as friend. By observing only global self-concept, which is many-faceted and contains diverse, even conflicting subselves, investigators have overlooked the importance of these subselves. By comparison, the Key research limited itself to the situation-specific self-concept that relates most closely to school success or failure: self-concept as learner.

Four factors that apparently relate significantly to school performance were derived through factor analysis in the Key research. These factors were labeled: (1) relating, (2) asserting, (3) investing, and (4) coping. Examination of these four factors in detail will be useful, for they serve as a basis for suggesting ways in which teachers may invite students to learning.

RELATING

> The highest expression of civilization is not its art but the supreme tenderness that people are strong enough to feel and show toward one another.
>
> **Norman Cousins** Editorial *Saturday Review*
> (1971)

The quality identified on the Key as having the greatest significance to self-concept as learner is *relating*. As measured by the Key, the relating score indicates the level of trust that the student maintains toward others.

Students who score high in relating identify closely with classmates, teachers, and school. They express positive feelings about learning, and they think in terms of *my* school, *our* teachers, and *my* classmates (as opposed to *the* teacher, *that* school, or *those* kids). Getting along with others is easy for those who score high on relating; thus they are able to take a natural, relaxed approach to school life. They are likely to stay calm when things go wrong, and they can express feelings of frustration or impatience without exploding.

Students who score low on relating seem unable to involve themselves in school activities or with teachers and other students. One teacher depicted such a student as follows:

> Two summers ago, I tutored children who were having problems learning to read. Looking back, I can see how their reading problems were related to how they saw themselves. One boy, John, who was ten years old, was not well-liked because of his habit of criticizing others to make himself feel important. His poor self-concept and failure to relate to others were graphically illustrated one day when a huge whipped cream fight was held on an empty hilltop. Whipped cream filled the air for 20 minutes or so as 40 kids, each with 2—3 cans, went wild. After the cream had settled, and later that day, John told me he had to spray whipped cream on himself as no one else made a point of doing so.

To be uninvited, even in a whipped cream battle, can be a most painful experience.

To be ignored by their peer group is an intolerable situation for most students, and most will go to great lengths to gain acceptance. When the desire for positive human relationships is unfulfilled in conventional ways, students are likely to try less conventional or socially unacceptable ways. For example, according to Cartwright, Tomson, and Schwartz (1975), Fitts and Hamner (1969), and others, the potential delinquent joins a gang to gain a feeling of status denied by the larger society.

The following passage from *Manchild in the Promised Land* by Claude

Brown (1965, p. 55) illustrates the pathetic efforts of one young girl to buy human relationships:

> I found out that Sugar would bring candy and pickles to class and give them to Carole, so Carole liked her and wanted me to like her too. After I got used to Sugar being ugly and having buckteeth, I didn't mind her always hanging around, and I stopped beating her up. Sugar started coming around on the weekends, and she always had money and wanted to take me to the show. Sometimes I would go with Sugar, and sometimes I would just take her money and go with somebody else. Most of the time I would take Sugar's money then find Bucky and take him to the show. Sugar used to cry, but I don't think she really minded it too much, because she knew she was ugly and had to have something to give people if she wanted them to like her. I never could get rid of Sugar. She would follow me around all day long and would keep trying to give me things, and when I didn't take them, she would start looking real pitiful and say she didn't want me to have it anyway. The only way I could be nice to Sugar was to take everything she had, so I started being real nice to her.

From literary descriptions as well as scientific research, it is clear that peer relationships have significant influence on both self-concept (Maehr, Mensing, and Nafeger, 1962) and school achievement (Damico, 1974, 1976).

While forcing students to relate to each other in positive and productive ways is probably impossible, teachers can create an inviting atmosphere in which relating is encouraged. A specific teacher behavior that invites feelings of belonging in students is the use of "we" statements to suggest group membership, encouraging students to involve themselves in school activities that become *our* curriculum, *our* decorations, *our* rules, *our* efforts to keep things clean. Instructional material can be developed and presented in such a way that students play an important part. Relating is also encouraged by the teacher's use of student names at every opportunity. Reis (1972) has provided a series of techniques for teachers who have a hard time remembering names.

Finally, creation of the proper atmosphere for relating involves the removal of barriers. Particular skill is necessary, as Haskins and Butts (1973)

K

Katz, P., & Zeigler, E. Self-image disparity: A developmental approach. *Journal of Personality and Social Psychology,* 1967, *5,* 186—195.

Keen, E. *Psychology and the new consciousness.* Monterey, Calif.: Brooks/Cole, 1972.

Kelley, H. H. The process of causal attribution. *American Psychologist,* 1973, *28,* 127—128.

Kelly, G. *Theory of personality: The psychology of personal constructs.* New York: Norton Library, 1963.

Kerlinger, F. N. *Foundations of behavioral research* (2nd ed.). New York: Holt, Rinehart and Winston, 1973.

Kesey, K. *One flew over the cuckoo's nest.* New York: Viking Press, 1962.

Kester, S. The communication of teacher expectations and their effects on the achievement and attitude of secondary school students. *American Educational Research Journal,* 1972, *66,* 51—58.

Kirschenbaum, H., Simon, S., & Napier, R. *Wad-ja-get? The grading game in American education.* New York: Hart, 1971.

Kraft, A. *The living classroom: Putting humanistic education into practice.* New York: Harper & Row, 1975.

Kranz, P. L., Weber, W. A., & Fishell, K. N. *The relationships between teacher perception of pupils and teacher behavior toward those pupils.* Paper presented at American Educational Research Association Convention, Minneapolis, 1970.

L

Landry, R. G. *Achievement and self concept: A curvilinear relationship.* Paper presented at American Educational Research Association Convention, Chicago, 1974.

Landry, R. G., & Edeburn, C. E. *Teacher self-concept and student self-concept.* Paper presented at American Educational Research Association Convention, Chicago, 1974.

Lanzetta, J. T., & Hannah, J. E. Reinforcing behavior of "naive" trainers. *Journal of Personality and Social Psychology,* 1969, *11,* 245—252.

LaVoie, J. C., & Adams, G. R. Teacher expectancy and its relation to physical and interpersonal characteristics of the child. *Alberta Journal of Educational Research,* 1974, *20*(2), 26—31.

Lazarus, R., & Averill, J. Emotion and cognition: With special reference to anxiety. In C. Speilberger (Ed.), *Anxiety: Current trends in theory and research* (Vol. 2). New York: Academic Press, 1972.

Lecky, P. *Self-consistency: A theory of personality.* New York: Island Press, 1945.

Lederer, J. The scope of the practice. *Urban Review,* 1968, *3,* 4—7.

Lefcourt, H. M. *Locus of control: Current trends in theory and research.* Hillsdale, N.J.: Erlbaum, 1976.

Lepper, M. R., & Greene, D. Turning play into work: Effects of adult surveillance and extrinsic rewards on children's intrinsic motivation. *Journal of Personality and Social Psychology,* 1975, *31,* 479—486.

Levin, D. *Soviet education today.* New York: John De Graff, 1959.

Levine, F. M., & Fasnacht, G. Token rewards may lead to token learning. *American Psychologist,* 1974, *29,* 816—820.

Lewin, K. *A dynamic theory of personality.* New York: McGraw-Hill, 1935.

Lewis, H. G., & Purkey, W. W. *Factories or families? Contrasting perceptions of the "good" school.* Unpublished manuscript, University of Florida, 1978.

Lippitt, R., & Gold, M. Classroom social structures as a mental health problem. *Journal of Social Issues,* 1959, *15,* 40—50.

Lippitt, R., & White, R. *Autocracy and democracy.* New York: Harper, 1960.

Liska, A. E. (Ed.). *The consistency controversy: Readings on the impact of attitude on behavior.* New York: Wiley, 1975.

Long, B. H., & Henderson, E. H. Certain determinants of academic expectancies among Southern and non-Southern teachers. *American Educational Research Journal,* 1974, *11*(2), 137—147.

Lorber, N. M. Inadequate social acceptance and disruptive classroom behavior. *Journal of Educational Research,* 1966, *59,* 360—362.

Ludwig, D. J., & Maehr, M. L. Changes in self-concept and stated behavioral preferences. *Child Development,* 1967, *38*(2), 453—467.

Luft, J. On nonverbal interaction. *Journal of Psychology,* 1966, *63*(2), 261—268.

Lynch, P. D., & Barnette, J. J. *An intervention to assist teachers in creating suppor-*

tive classroom climates. Paper presented at American Educational Research Association Convention, New York, 1977.

M

Maccoby, E. E., Newcomb, T. M., & Hartley, E L. (Eds.). *Readings in social psychology.* New York: Holt, Rinehart and Winston, 1958.

Madsen, C. H., Madsen, C. K., Sandargas, R. A., Hammond, W. R., & Edgar, D. E. *Classroom RAID (rules, approval, ignore, disapproval): A cooperative approach for professionals and volunteers.* Unpublished manuscript, University of Florida, 1970.

Maehr, M. L. *Sociocultural origins of achievement.* Monterey, Calif.: Brooks/Cole, 1974.

Maehr, M. L., Mensing, J., & Nafeger, S. Concept of self and the reaction of others. *Sociometry,* 1962, *25,* 353—357.

Mahaffey, L. L., Brophy, J. E., & Evertson, C. *Teacher feedback to childrens' answers: Process-product relationships.* Paper presented at American Educational Research Association Convention, Washington, D.C., 1975.

Maher, G. *Clinical psychology and personality: The selected papers of George Kelly.* New York: Wiley, 1969.

Mahoney, M. J. *Cognition and behavior modification.* Cambridge, Mass.: Ballinger, 1974.

Mahoney, M. J. The sensitive scientist in empirical humanism. *American Psychologist,* 1975, *30,* 864—867.

Malpass, L. F. Some relationships between students' perceptions of school and achievement. *Journal of Educational Psychology,* 1954, *44,* 475—482.

Manning, J. Discipline in the good old days. *Phi Delta Kappan,* 1959, *41*(3), 87—91.

Marrow, A. J., Bowers, D. G., & Seashore, S. E. *Management by participation.* New York: Harper & Row, 1967.

Marshall, M. Self evaluation in seventh grade. *Elementary School Journal,* 1960, *60,* 249—252.

Maslow, A. H. Personality problems and personality growth. In C. Moustakas (Ed.), *The self: Explorations in personal growth.* New York: Harper, 1956.

Maslow, A. H. *The psychology of science: A reconnaissance.* Chicago: Henry Regnery, 1969.

Maslow, A. H. *Motivation and personality* (2nd ed.). New York: Harper & Row, 1970.

Masters, E. L. *Spoon River anthology.* New York: Macmillan, 1935.

May, R. *Man's search for himself.* New York: Norton, 1953.

May, R. D. *Students turned-off by school.* Unpublished manuscript, Guidance Service Section, Pennsylvania Department of Education, 1976.

Mayeske, G. W., Wisler, C. E., Beaton, A. E., Jr., Weinfield, F. D., Cohen, W. M., Okada, T., Proshek, J. M., & Tabler, D. A. *A study of our nation's schools.* Washington, D.C.: U.S. Government Printing Office, 1972.

McGinley, P., & McGinley, H. Reading groups as psychological groups. *Journal of Experimental Education,* 1970, *39,* 36—42.

McKeachee, W. J. The decline and fall of the laws of learning. *Educational Researcher, 3*(1), 1974, 48—64.

McKusick, V. A. *Mendelian inheritance in man* (3rd ed.). Baltimore: Johns Hopkins Press, 1971.

Mead, G. H. *Mind, self and society.* Chicago: University of Chicago Press, 1934.

Medley, D. M., & Mitzel, H. E. Some behavioral correlates of teacher effectiveness. *Journal of Educational Psychology,* 1959, *50,* 239—246.

Mehrabian, A. *Tactics of social influence.* Englewood Cliffs, N.J.: Prentice-Hall, 1970.

Mehrabian, A. *Silent messages.* Belmont, Calif.: Wadsworth, 1971.

Mehrabian, A. *Nonverbal communication.* Chicago: Aldine-Atherton, 1972.

Meichenbaum, D., Bowers, K., & Ross, J. A behavioral analysis of teacher expectancy effect. *Journal of Personality and Social Psychology,* 1969, *13,* 306—316.

Meichenbaum, D. *Cognitive behavior modification* (University Programs Modular Studies). Morristown, N.J.: General Learning Press, 1974.

Meichenbaum, D., Gilmore, B., & Fedoravicius, A. Group insight versus group desensitization in treating speech anxiety. *Journal of Consulting and Clinical Psychology,* 1971, *36,* 410—421.

Mendels, G. E., & Flanders, J. P. Teachers' expectations and pupil performance. *American Educational Research Journal,* 1973, *10*(3), 203—212.

Mettee, D. R. Rejection of unexpected success as function of the negative consequences of accepting success. *Journal of Personality and Social Psychology,*
1971, *71,* 332—341.

Mizer, J. E. Cipher in the snow. *NEA Journal,* 1964, *53,* 8—10.

Morse, W. C. Self-concept in the school setting. *Childhood Education,* 1964, *41,*
195—198.

Moustakas, C. E. *The authentic teacher: Sensitivity and awareness in the classroom.*
Cambridge, Mass.: Howard A. Doyle, 1966.

Murphey, G. *Personality.* New York: Harper & Row, 1947.

Murphy, G., & Spohn, H. E. *Encounter with reality.* Boston: Houghton Mifflin,
1968.

N

Neff, F. Performance-based teaching—a new orthodoxy? In J. J. Jelinek (Ed.),
Performance-based criteria for teacher education. Tempe, Ariz.: Arizona ASCD,
Bureau of Educational Research, Arizona State Universtiy, 1973.

Newman, M., & Berkowitz, B. *How to be your own best friend.* New York: Ballan-
tine Books, 1971.

Niemeyer, J. Some guidelines to desirable elementary school reorganization. In *Programs for the educationally disadvantaged.* Washington, D.C.: U.S. Office of
Education (Bulletin no. 17, 1963).

Norman, R. V. School administration: Thoughts on organization and purpose. *Phi
Delta Kappan,* 1966, 47, 315—316.

Notz, W. W. Work motivation and the negative effects of extrinsic rewards: A review
with implications for theory and practice. *American Psychologist,* 1975, *30*(9),
884—891.

O

O'Roark, A. M. *A comparison of the perceptual characteristics of elected legislators
and public school counselors identified as most and least effective.* Unpublished doctoral dissertation, University of Florida, 1974.

Owen, E. H. *A comparison of disadvantaged and non-disadvantaged elementary
school pupils on two measures of self-concept as learner.* Unpublished doctoral
dissertation, University of Florida, 1972.

P

Palardy, J. What teachers believe, what children achieve. *Elementary School Journal,* 1969, *69,* 370—374.

Parker, J. The relationship of self-report to inferred self-concept. *Journal of Educational and Psychological Measurement,* 1966, *26,* 691—700.

Patterson, C. H. The self in recent Rogerian theory. *Journal of Individual Psychology,* 1961, *17,* 5—11.

Patterson, C. H. *Humanistic education.* Englewood Cliffs, N.J.: Prentice-Hall, 1973.

Peck, R. F., Fox, R. B., & Marston, P. T. *Teacher effects on student achievement and self-esteem.* Paper presented at American Educational Research Association Convention, New York, 1977.

Pedulla, J., Airasian, P., Madaus, G., & Kellaghan, T. *Shifts in teacher ratings of students resulting from standardized test scores.* Paper presented at American Educational Research Association Convention, New York, 1977.

Pellegrini, R., & Hicks, R. Prophecy errects and tutorial instructions for the disadvantaged child. *American Educational Research Journal,* 1972, *9,* 413—420.

Peng, S. S. *Teacher class-expectations, instructional behaviors, and pupil achievement.* Paper presented at American Educational Research Association Convention, Chicago, 1974.

Pennock, C. D. *Student teacher expectations for primary level boys' reading achievement.* Unpublished doctoral dissertation, University of Illinois, 1971.

Phares, E. J. *Locus of control in personality.* Morristown, N.J.: General Learning Press, 1976.

Plato. *The dialogues of Plato* (4th ed.). Trans. B. Jowett. Oxford: Clarendon Press, 1973.

Polanyi, M. *The tacit dimension.* New York: Doubleday, 1966.

Prather, H. *Notes to myself.* Lafayette, Calif.: Real People Press, 1970.

Pullias, E. V. *A common sense philosophy for modern man.* New York: Philosophical Library, 1975.

Purkey, W. W. *Self-concept and school achievement.* Englewood Cliffs, N.J.: Prentice-Hall, 1970.

Purkey, W. W. The invitational secondary school. *Thresholds in Secondary Education,* 1975, *3,* 16—19.

Purkey, W. W. Invitations from Mr. Jefferson. *Proceedings, University of Virginia Education Day,* 1976a.

Purkey, W. W. Powerful invitations in education. *Iowa Association for School, College, and University Newsletter.* University of Iowa, October 1976b.

Purkey, W. W. The bell invites me. *Proceedings, Mathematics '76.* York University, Ontario, 1976c.

Purkey, W. W., & Avila, D. L. Classroom discipline: A self-concept approach. *Elementary School Journal,* 1971, *6*, 325—328.

Purkey, W. W., Cage, B., & Graves, W. The Florida Key: A scale to infer learner self-concept, *Journal of Educational and Psychological Measurement,* 1973, *33*, 979—984.

Purkey, W. W., Graves, W., & Zellner, M. Self-perceptions of pupils in an experimental elementary school. *Elementary School Journal,* 1970, *71*, 166—171.

R

Raimy, V. C. Self-reference in counseling interviews. *Journal of Consulting Psychology,* 1948, *12*, 153—163.

Raskin, M. *Being and doing.* New York: Random House, 1971.

Raths, L., Harmin, M., & Simon, S. *Values and teaching: Working with values in the classroom.* Columbus, Ohio: Charles E. Merrill, 1966.

Reckless, W. C., & Dinitz, S. Pioneering with self concept as a vulnerability factor in delinquency. *Journal of Criminal Law, Criminology and Police Science,* 1967. *58*, 515—523.

Reeves, J. W. *Body and mind in Western thought.* Baltimore: Penguin Books, 1958.

Reis, R. Learning your students' names. *Education,* 1972, *93*, 45—46.

Richards, A. C., & Richards, F. Goals of educational psychology in teacher education: A humanistic perspective. Paper presented at American Educational Research Association Convention, Washington, D.C., 1975.

Rimm, D. C., & Litvak, S. B. Self-verbalization and emotional arousal. *Journal of Abnormal Psychology,* 1969, *74*, 181—187.

Rist, R. C. Student social class and teacher expectations: The self fulfilling prophecy in ghetto education. *Harvard Educational Review,* 1970, *40*, 411—451.

Rogers, C. R. Some observations on the organization of personality. *American Psychologist,* 1947, *2,* 358—368.

Rogers, C. R. *Client-centered therapy.* Boston: Houghton Mifflin, 1951.

Rogers, C. R. The therapeutic relationship: Recent theory and research. *Australian Journal of Psychology,* 1965, *17*(5), 95—108.

Rogers, C. R. *Coming into existence.* New York: World Publishing Co., 1967.

Rogers, C. R. Forget you are a teacher: Carl Rogers tells why. *Instructor,* 1971, *81*(1), 65—67.

Rogers, C. R. My philosophy of interpersonal relationships and how it grew. *Journal of Humanistic Psychology,* 1973, *13*(2), 12—19.

Rogers, C. R. In retrospect—forty-six years. *American Psychologist,* 1974, *29*(2), 115.

Rogers, C. R. The interpersonal relationship in the facilitation of learning. In R. R. Leeper (Ed.), *Humanizing education: The person in the process.* Washington, D.C.: Association for Supervision and Curriculum Development, 1976.

Rosenberg, M. J. *Society and the adolescent self image.* Princeton, N.J.: Princeton University Press, 1965.

Rosenberg, M. J. Discussion: The concepts of self. In R. P. Abelson et al. (Eds.). *Theories of congitive consistency: A sourcebook.* Chicago: Rand McNally, 1968.

Rosenhan, D. L. On being sane in insane places. *Science,* 1973, *179,* 250—258.

Rosenshine, B. Enthusiastic teaching: A research review. *School Review,* 1970a, *72,* 499—514.

Rosenshine, B. Evaluation of classroom instruction. *Review of Educational Research,* 1970b, *40,* 279—300.

Rosenshine, B. *Teaching behaviours and student achievement.* London: N.E.F.R., 1971.

Rosenshine, B. & McGaw, B. Issues in assessing teacher accountability in public education. *Phi Delta Kappan,* 1972, *43,* 640—643.

Rosenthal, R., & Jacobson, L. Teacher expectations for the disadvantaged. *Scientific American,* 1968a, *218,* 19—23.

Rosenthal, R., & Jacobson, L. *Pygmalion in the classroom: Teacher expectation and pupils' intellectual development.* New York: Holt, Rinehart and Winston, 1968b.

Rosenthal, R., & Rubin, D. Pygmalion reaffirmed. In J. Elashoff & R. Snow, *Pygmal-*

ion reconsidered. A case study in statistical inference: Reconsideration of the Rosenthal-Jacobson data on teacher expectancy. Worthington, Ohio: Charles A. Jones, 1971.

Rothbart, M., Dalfen, S., & Barrett, R. Effects of teacher's expectancy on student-teacher interaction. *Journal of Educational Psychology,* 1971, *62*, 49—54.

Rowe, M. B. Wait-time and rewards as instructional variables, their influence on language, logic and fate-control: Part I: Wait-time. *Journal of Research in Science Teaching,* 1974a, *2*(2), 81—94.

Rowe, M. B. Reflections on wait-time: Some methodological questions. *Journal of Research in Science Teaching,* 1974b, *11*(3), 263—279.

Rowe, M. B. Relation of wait-time and rewards to the development of language, logic and fate control: Part II: Rewards. *Journal of Research in Science Teaching,* 1974c, *11*(4), 290—308.

Rubin, L. J. *Facts and feelings in the classroom.* New York: Viking Press, 1973.

Rubovits, P., & Maehr, M. Pygmalion analyzed: Toward an explanation of the Rosenthal-Jacobson findings. *Journal of Personality and Social Psychology,* 1971, *19*, 197—203.

S

Sabine, G. A. *How students rate their schools and teachers.* Washington, D.C.: National Association of Secondary School Principals, 1971.

Sargent, S. Humanistic methodology in personality and social psychology. In J. F. T. Bugental (Ed.), *Challenges of humanistic psychology.* New York: McGraw-Hill, 1967.

School suspensions: Are they helping children? Children's Defense Fund, Washington Research Project, Inc., Cambridge, Mass., 1975.

Schrank, W. R. The labeling effect of ability grouping. *Journal of Educational Research,* 1968, *62*, 51—52.

Schrank, W. R. Further study of the labeling effects of ability—grouping. *Journal of Educational Research,* 1970, *63*, 358—360.

Sears, P., & Feldman, D. Teacher interactions. *National Elementary Principal,* 1966, *46*, 30—36.

Seaver, W. B. Effects of naturally induced teacher expectancies. *Journal of Personality and Social Psychology,* 1973, *28*, 333—342.

Seligman, M. E. *Helplessness: On depression, development, and death.* San Francisco: Freeman, 1975.

Shakow, D. What is clinical psychology? *American Psychologist,* 1976, *31,* 553—560.

Shavelson, R., Hubner, J., & Stanton, G. Self-concept: Validation of construct interpretations. *Review of Educational Research,* 1976, *46*(3), 407—441.

Shaw, G. B. *The devil's disciple.* In *Nine plays.* New York: Dodd, Mead, 1935.

Shaw, G. B. *Pygmalion.* New York: Dodd, Mead, 1940.

Silberman, C. E. *Crisis in the classroom.* New York: Random House, 1970.

Simon, S., Howe, L., & Kirschenbaum, H. *Values clarification: A handbook of practical strategies for teachers and students.* New York: Hart, 1972.

Skinner, B. F. *Beyond freedom and dignity.* New York: Knopf, 1971.

Sloan, H. N. *Classroom management: Remediation and prevention.* New York: Wiley, 1976.

Smith, B. O. *Teachers for the real world.* Washington, D.C.: American Association of Colleges for Teacher Education, 1970.

Snow, R. E. Unfinished Pygmalion. *Contemporary Psychology,* 1969, *14,* 197—199.

Snygg, D., & Combs, A. W. *Individual behavior.* New York: Harper & Row, 1949.

Soar, R. S. Teacher-pupil interaction. In J. Squirre (Ed.), *1972 A. S. C. D. Yearbook: A new look at progressive education.* Washington, D.C.: A. S. C. D., 1972.

Soares, A. T., & Soares, L. M. Interpersonal and self-perceptions of disadvantaged high school students. *Proceedings of 78th Annual Convention of American Psychological Association,* 1970, *5*(1), 457—458.

Spaulding, R. L. *Achievement, creativity, and self concept correlates of teacher-pupil transactions in elementary schools* (USOE Cooperative Research Report No. 1352). Urbana: University of Illinois, 1963.

Spears, W. D., & Deese, M. E. Self concept as cause. *Educational Theory,* 1973, *23*(2), 144—153.

Staines, J. W. The self-picture as a factor in the classroom. *British Journal of Educational Psychology,* 1958, *28,* 97—111.

Stanwyck, D. J., & Felker, D. W. *Self-concept and anxiety in middle elementary school children: A developmental survey.* Paper presented at American Educational Research Association Convention, Chicago, 1974.

Stevens, D. O. Reading difficulty and classroom acceptance. *The Reading Teacher,* 1971, *25,* 197—199.

Stevenson, H. W. *Children's learning.* New York: Appleton-Century-Crofts, 1972.

Sunby, D. Y. *The relationship of teacher-child perception similarities and teacher-ratings, and the effect of children's self-perceptions and teacher-rating.* Unpublished doctoral dissertation, Purdue University, 1971.

Swift, J. *Gulliver's travels.* New York: Macmillan, 1962.

Szasz, T. *Heresies.* Garden City, N.Y.: Anchor Books, 1976.

T

Tagiuri, R., Bruner, J. S., & Blake, R. R. On the relation between feelings and perception of feelings among members of small groups. In E. E. Maccoby, T. M. Newcomb, & E. L. Hartley (Eds.), *Readings in social psychology.* New York: Holt, Rinehart and Winston, 1958.

Taylor, C. The expectations of Pygmalion's creators. *Educational Leadership,* 1970, *28,* 161—165.

Taylor, M. *Intercorrelations among three methods of estimating students' attention.* Stanford, Calif.: Stanford Center for Research on Teaching, 1968.

Taylor, R. G. Personality traits and discrepant achievement: A review. *Journal of Counseling Psychology,* 1964, *11,* 76—81.

Thorndike, R. L. Review of *Pygmalion in the classroom* by R. Rosenthal & L. Jacobson. *American Educational Research Journal,* 1968, *5,* 708—711.

Tjosvold, D. Alternative organizations for schools and classrooms. In D. Bartel & L. Saxe (Eds.), *Social psychology of education: Research and theory.* New York: Hemisphere Press, 1977.

Tjosvold, D., & Santamaria, P. *The effects of cooperation and teacher support on student attitudes toward classroom decision-making.* Paper presented at American Educational Research Convention, New York, 1977.

Tome, H. R. *Le moi et l'autre dans la conscience de l'adolescent (The self and the other person in the consciousness of the adolescent).* Neuchatel, Switzerland: Delachaux & Niestle, 1972.

Trent, R. D. The relationship between expressed self-acceptance and expressed attitudes toward Negro and white in Negro children. *Journal of Genetic Psychology,* 1957, *91*, 25—31.

Trexler, L. D., & Karst, T. O. Rational-emotive therapy, placebo, and no treatment effects on public speaking anxiety. *Journal of Abnormal Psychology,* 1972, *79*, 60—67.

Tyo, A. M. *A comparison of the verbal behavior of teachers in interaction with migrant and non-migrant students.* Genesco, N.Y.: State University of New York, 1972. (ERIC Document Reproduction Service No. 075-160)

U

Usher, R., & Hanke, J. The "third force" in psychology and college teacher effectiveness research at the University of Northern Colorado. *Colorado Journal of Educational Research,* 1971, *10*(2), 3—10.

V

Veltin, E. A laboratory task for induction of mood states. *Behaviour Research and Therapy,* 1968, *6*, 475—482.

Videback, E. The effect of self esteem on romantic liking. *Journal of Experimental and Social Psychology,* 1965, *1*, 184—197.

W

Wagoner, J. L., Jr. *Thomas Jefferson and the education of a new nation.* Bloomington, Ind.: Phi Delta Kappa Educational Foundation, 1976.

Wallen, N. E., & Travers, R. M. W. Analysis and investigation of teacher methods. In N. L. Gage (Ed.), *Handbook of research on teaching.* Chicago: Rand McNally, 1963.

Wasicsko, M. *Development of a research-based teacher selection instrument.* Unpublished doctoral dissertation, University of Florida, 1977.

Watson, J. B. *Behaviorism.* New York: Norton, 1925.

Webster, M., & Sobieszek, B. *Sources of self-evaluation: A formal theory of significant others and social influence.* New York: Wiley, 1974.

Wheeler, R., & Ryan, F. Effects of cooperative and competitive classroom environments on the attitudes and achievement of elementary school students engaged in social studies inquiry activities. *Journal of Educational Psychology,* 1973, *65,* 402—407.

Whimbey, A., & Whimbey, L. *Intelligence can be taught.* New York: Dutton, 1975.

White, R. K., & Lippitt, R. *Autocracy and democracy: An experimental inquiry.* New York: Harper, 1960.

White, R. W. Motivation reconsidered: The concept of competence. *Psychological Review,* 1959, *66,* 297—333.

Whitt, R. *Attitudes of teachers in relation to student self concept and attitudes toward school.* Unpublished doctoral dissertation, Wayne State University, 1966.

Wilkins, W. E. *Teacher expectations and classroom behaviors.* Paper presented at American Educational Research Association Convention, Chicago, 1974.

Wilkins, W. E., & Glock, M. D. *Teacher expectations and student achievement: A replication and extension.* Ithaca, N.Y.: Cornell University, 1973. (ERIC Document Reproduction Service No. 080-567.

Williams, R., & Kamala, A. *Cooperative classroom discipline.* Columbus, Ohio: Charles E. Merrill, 1973.

Williams, R. L., & Cole, S. Self-concept and school adjustment. *Personnel and Guidance Journal,* 1958, *46,* 478—481.

Willis, B. J. The influence of teacher expectation on teachers' classroom interaction with selected children. *Dissertation Abstracts International,* 1970, *30*(11-A), 5072.

Witkins, H. A., Dyk, R. B., Foterson, H. F., Goodenough, D. R., & Karp, S. A. *Psychological differentiation.* New York: Wiley, 1962.

Woolfolk, R. L., & Woolfolk, A. E. Effects of teacher verbal and nonverbal behaviors on student perceptions and attitudes. *American Educational Research Journal,* 1974, *11,* 297—303.

Wylie, R. C. *The self-concept.* Lincoln: University of Nebraska Press, 1961.

Wylie, R. C. *The self-concept* (Vol. I, rev. ed.). Lincoln: University of Nebraska Press, 1974.

Wyne, M. D., White, K. P., & Coop, R. H. *The black self.* Englewood Cliffs, N.J.: Prentice-Hall, 1974.

Y

Yamamoto, K., Thomas, E. C., & Karnes, E. A. School related attitudes in middle-school age students. *American Educational Research Journal,* 1969, *6,* 191—206.

Yeatts, P. P. Developmental changes in the self-concept of children grades 3—12. Gainesville: *Florida Educational Research and Development Council Research Bulletin,* 1967, *3,* 2.

Z

Ziller, R. C. *The social self.* New York: Pergamon Press, 1973.

Zimbardo, P. G. The human choice: Individuation, reason, and order versus deindividuation, impulse, and chaos. In W. J. Arnold & D. Levine (Eds.), *Nebraska symposium on motivation.* Lincoln: University of Nebraska Press, 1969.

Zimmerman, I. L., & Allebrand, G. N. Personality characteristics and attitudes toward achievement of good and poor readers. *Journal of Educational Research,* 1965, *59*(1), 28—30.

INDEX